GIFTS OF MEDITATION

9 Steps for Your Journey to Inner Peace

MICHAEL J. DAWSON

for Samantha

Acknowledgements

I write in gratitude to Victoria for the

constancy of her love and support and

for her editorial input, to Jerry for his

wise guidance, to Keoki for his insight

and for encouraging me to speak from

the heart, to Guy for always being there

and to my Mother for inspiring me

never to "rest on my laurels."

"Sitting quietly

Doing nothing

Spring comes

And the grass grows by itself."

Introduction

The world is full enough of books offering instruction on how to meditate. The last thing I ever wanted was to add my voice to the long list of those involved in such endeavors.

I moved to Maui a few short years ago anticipating a time of quiet retirement from the pressures of survival in the big city and then, quite suddenly, everything shifted. I went through an unexpected yet unavoidable divorce and found myself feeling alone and isolated on this luscious green island in the middle of a vast blue ocean.

I reflected upon the singular journey of my life and the apparently random meetings with remarkable beings which guided and directed me to the many practices that have sustained me along the way. I finally arrived at the startling realization that it was, and is, incumbent upon me to share these great and life-affirming gifts, woven within the personal history that gave rise to them.

My purpose here is not to teach but rather to inspire, and I address myself not only to beginners on the path, but also to those who know full well how much can be gained from sitting and breathing for a few minutes each day and who, perhaps, could use a reminder or a little encouragement. The practice of meditation is, after all is said and done, primarily an act of will.

It is challenging to speak from the heart. The poetry of our spirits is overwhelmed by the thoughts and cares of a trillion trivialities.

This small book is an attempt to speak from the heart and to find meaning and purpose in my own pilgrimage.

"The centipede was happy, quite

 Until a toad, in fun, asked,

"Pray which leg goes after which?"

 This worked his mind to such a pitch

 He lay distracted in a ditch

 Considering how to run."

Chapter One

Zen and the Art of Mindless Meditation

I was born into a family of Jewish migrants who fled from religious persecution in Eastern Europe towards the end of the 19th century and all 4 of my grandparents were born and raised in England in the Orthodox tradition.

The emotional climax to the Sabbath service touched the core of my being before I can even remember:

The scrolls have been held aloft for all to see, wrapped in silk, decorated with silver, paraded down the aisle and lovingly kissed. They lie in the Ark now, under glowing lights. We are on our feet singing the Hebrew scripture in joyful union:

"It is the Tree of Life to those that hold fast to it. Its roots are happiness, its arteries are sweetness and all its branches are peace. Return us, Lord, to You, And we will get back to where we once belonged."

Tears fill my eyes and I am transported into the Mystery.

My parents were prominent in our community and although I continually rebelled against all rules and restrictions, I received the blessed gift of a spiritual foundation from which to build my own pathway back to that blissful state.

I was sent, much against my will, to a religious Jewish high school for boys, and graduated firm in the conviction that I would always be a non-believer, yet I invariably felt like an outsider looking in on the peculiarly detached English way of being.

I had learned to play the part of an educated gentleman quite well, earning a degree in Business Administration, drinking excessive amounts of alcohol, smoking a pack-a-day, working in the London stock market, wearing 3-piece pinstriped suits and a starched white collar, carrying the obligatory rolled umbrella, reading *The Financial Times* and playing golf. All I was missing was the bowler hat and the masonic handshake, but I was secretly praying for deliverance from the monotony, conformity, and crush of city life.

I was always a restless spirit. By the time I was out of my teens, I had bicycled, flown, hitchhiked, ridden the rails and driven all across the European continent, sometimes with school friends but mostly alone, from Spain to Czechoslovakia and from Sweden to Yugoslavia, spouting schoolboy French, German and Italian.

In 1970, as a 22 year old, I spent some time in Israel, searching for my inner identity as a secular Jew and, at first, stayed in an apartment in Jerusalem with an old school friend and a couple of brainy American girls who were university librarians from Boston. These were the first Americans I had spent any time with and I was fascinated to hear them talk openly about visits to their psychotherapists. It had never occurred to me that "normal" people even experienced an inner process, let alone that they actually self-reflected. I thought only crazy people had their heads examined. What did I know?

I was inspired to begin a reconnaissance of my own inner landscape and started to write a daily journal.

One of the girls had developed a familiar friendship with the jovial *Roshi* (Head Monk) of the local Japanese Zen Buddhist Monastery who once came to visit. His English wasn't very good but his eyes sparkled, he laughed a lot and, over tea, he gave me a book called "The Way of Zen" by Alan Watts, an English-born Episcopalian priest who, in the late 1950s, began interpreting and popularizing Buddhism for the Western audience and lived on a houseboat in Sausalito, California.

I stayed up all night, finished the book, and felt as though the top of my head had been blown open. My mind had been extracted from the tangle it found itself in, as a result of confusing words and ideas with reality and I was suddenly, inexplicable free.

We drove to a big old house in the Arab Quarter of the city every Wednesday afternoon throughout a wet and windy winter. The main room was spacious with faded red carpets covering the grey cement floor and a cold draft blowing in under the door from the noisy street outside. About a dozen of us sat on cushions in a circle, facing outwards, staring at the bare painted walls and counting our breaths, while the *Roshi* patrolled the center carrying two small blocks of wood. If he found you slouching, slumping or sleeping he would bang them together just behind your head. That would do it!

We sat for 3 cycles of 30 minutes, which were interrupted by 2 short walking meditations. I learned discipline and focus which served me well on the road ahead.

Practice: The Threefold Calming Breath

In 1950s, before the arrival of central heating, Londoners closed their windows and lit coal fires as the freeze of late autumn descended. The fog, much romanticized in literature and song was, in fact, coal dust and I walked and ran the 2 miles to and from elementary school, sometimes unable to see even the edge of the pavement. As a 9-year-old I succumbed to bronchial asthma and spent 2 winters in bed hallucinating feverishly.

My mother had the good sense to override the doctor's advice that I rely on inhalers and took me to a naturopathic clinic where they prescribed a vegetarian diet, massage and breathing exercises. I was completely cured, and I believe I owe my intuitive gift for bodywork and my healthy lifestyle to the work

of those insightful practitioners of natural
medicine.

I recommend this breathing exercise for
insomnia and the relief of anxiety:

· Place one hand on the belly below the navel.
· Inhale to the count of 3 allowing the belly to
  fill completely.
· Exhale to the count of 3 contracting the belly
  and emptying the lungs.

· Place the other hand on the solar plexus just
  below the ribcage.
· Inhale to the count of 3 allowing the solar
  plexus to fill completely.
· Exhale to the count of 3, contracting the solar
  plexus and emptying the lungs.

· Inhale to the count of 3, allowing the chest to
  fill completely.
· Exhale to the count of 3, contracting the chest
  and emptying the lungs.

- *Now put the 3 breaths together into 1 long breath as you count to 9.*

- *Inhale as the belly expands to the count of 3, then the solar plexus expands to the count of 3, and then the chest expands to the count of 3, filling the lungs completely.*

- *Exhale as the chest contracts to the count of 3, the solar plexus contracts to the count of 3, the belly contracts to the count of 3 and the lungs empty completely.*

- *Repeat this long breath 9 times.*

Practice: Zazen Sitting Meditation

- *Turn your chair to the wall.*
- *Place your right hand gently inside your left, palms up, on your lap.*
- *Sit with your spine as erect as is comfortable and half-close your eye lids.*
- *Fix your eyes on a spot on the wall at about the level of your knees.*
- *Allow your eyes to cross very slightly and go out of focus.*

- *Breathe gently and become aware of the coolness of your breath as it enters your nostrils and its warmth as you exhale.*

- *Begin to count your breaths.*
- *Breathe in, breathe out, count 1. Breathe in, breathe out, count 2. Breathe in, breathe out, count 3............continue breathing and counting up to 10.*

- *After you reach 10 begin at 1 again. Keep repeating this process*

- *Each time you find your mind wandering or you go unconscious, or you simply lose track of where you are at, forgive yourself and return to the beginning, and breathe in, breathe out, count 1................*
- *Continue counting for 5 minutes.*

- *Rise from your sitting position and walk slowly, anti-clockwise around the room. As you step with your left foot state silently, "I have arrived." As you step with the right foot repeat, "I am home." Continue this walking meditation with affirmations for 2 minutes.*

- *Return to your seat and continue to breathe and count for 5 minutes.*
- *Walk for 2 minutes repeating the affirmation.*
- *Sit for 5 minutes more continuing to count and then end this meditation practice.*

GIFTS OF MEDITATION

"When one fixes the thought on the mid-point

Between the two eyes

The light streams in of its own accord."

Chapter Two

The Secret of the Golden Flower

I left Israel having ultimately recognized that I felt no compelling connection to that continuously contested strip of land, nor any particular desire to take on the unrelenting Israeli struggle as my own.

I did, however, continue to journal and I read the works of the founders of psychoanalysis, particularly Sigmund Freud and Carl Jung in an attempt to understand my own fears, fixations and frailties.

In Jung's autobiographical writings he mentions an ancient Chinese text called

"The Secret of the Golden Flower."
Through studying that book I developed
the practice of concentrating on opening
the 3rd (inner) eye, located in the middle of
the brow, just above the junction of the
eyebrows.

In the Eastern tradition that spot is
understood to be the doorway to the pineal
gland, a small pine cone shaped body in
the center of the brain which secretes the
hormone melatonin. It controls our sleep
and dream cycles and is known as "the seat
of the soul."

Practice: The Golden Flower Meditation

· Lay the tongue along the roof of the mouth.
· Breathe rhythmically through the nose.
· Close your eyes and focus them on the 3rd eye.
· Imagine a flower of golden light at the base of the spine. The light rises on the in-breath and falls on the out-breath.
· On the in-breath the light rises up the spine, moves forward across the top of the head and enters the 3rd eye.
· On the out-breath the light travels down the front of the body and back to the base of the spine.
· Resist the temptation to follow the light as it circulates and keep your attention focused on the middle of the forehead, just above the junction of the eyebrows.
· Continue to circulate the light for 20 minutes.

"The wild geese do not intend to cast

Their reflection.

The water has no mind to receive their image."

Chapter Three

The Sound of Silence

The next summer I was introduced to David. He was just a few years older than me, a blond, blue-eyed, rather posh English pilot who chain-smoked filterless French cigarettes, dressed like a WW2 flyer and did terrifying aerobatic stunts in his too-big-to-barrel-roll 8-seater twin turbo prop. He was an overseas agent for several British airport equipment manufacturers. He sold the tugs that pull airplanes and passenger steps, baggage handling carousels and flight information systems to the developing nations of Africa and the Middle East, and was looking for someone with a financial and sales background to travel with him and be his #2. I knew very little about airplanes at that time but we clicked, I was hired and moved into a rooftop apartment in Milan, Italy, close to where he had established his head office.

Our major focus turned out to be East African Airways and in Kenya he taught me how to fly a plane so that I could evolve into becoming his co-pilot on the long journeys in his smoke-filled cabin.

It was in Nairobi that I began to take classes in Transcendental Meditation (TM). The Maharishi Mahesh Yogi introduced TM into India in the 1950s and in the mid-60s he was discovered and popularized in the West by the Beatles. His technique is now practiced by over 6 million people worldwide.

The practice is a *mantra,* a word or chant which is chosen for you by the teacher of your class and whisper into your ear. When repeated silently in meditation, it is capable of creating transformation.

TM is practiced for 20 minutes twice a day, morning and evening, and I realized the calming benefits of commitment to a regular meditation schedule as my life grew increasingly chaotic.

I promised, all those years ago, never to reveal the *mantra* my teacher gave to me, but 2 of the most familiar and universal *mantras,* which I love to use, are:

- *A-U-M* (3 syllables of equal length representing Creation, Preservation and Liberation) and
- *Om Mani Padme Hum* (The Creation of The Jewel in the Lotus, the sacred flower of Buddhism).

Practice: A Mantra Meditation

- *Focus your closed eyes on the 3rd eye.*

- *Think of your mantra and repeat it slowly and quietly to yourself.*

- *Allow your thoughts to come and go as they will.*

- *Each time you become aware that you are not thinking of the mantra, feel compassion in your heart for your own process and return to the repetition of the chant.*

- *Continue for up to 20 minutes, then sit quietly and just breathe for 2 minutes before ending your practice.*

GIFTS OF MEDITATION

"I have no peace of mind."

"Bring out your mind before me and I will

pacify it."

"But when I seek my own mind I cannot

find it."

"There, I have pacified your mind."

Chapter Four

Grounded in Marin

David always drove himself really hard and our business was extremely successful but, after 3 years of working closely together, I noticed his frustration building and his behavior becoming increasingly erratic. I was experiencing some stress-related symptoms myself. I had eaten too much airline and hotel food, drunk copious quantities of alcohol and was smoking unceasingly. I quit, in the gentlest way I could manage, and joined some friends I knew from my days working in the stock market, who were in the fashion import-export business. I kept in touch with David, whose health had begun its decline, and by the end of the 1970s, he had died, still in his early-30s, of lung and, ultimately, brain cancer.

I devoted myself to my new venture and was working a trade show in Kensington Town Hall on a dreary Christmas Eve when, across the crowded room, I noticed Sally, an attractive young woman wearing ruby-red lipstick and a startlingly short skirt, modeling the latest clothing designs. We talked and she told me about a young man she had met at a recent photo shoot. On that day she was feeling particularly agitated and the photographer's assistant had put his hands on her shoulders and "calmed her right down." She asked him where he had learned to send healing energy like that and he told her about a man named Eric, a medium who preached at Spiritualist churches around town bringing messages to the bereaved from "the great beyond."

Sally had attended some of the weekly *seances* Eric held in the small terraced house he shared with his two teenage children and invited me to one of them. Eric took one look at me and told me I was a healer. It actually sounded something like, *"Yurnealer Moikul."* He would close the curtains, switch on a dim red light and enter a trance-like state, channeling messages to us from our guides and teachers.

There were 4 or 5 of us in our core group, and Eric led us in the laying-on of hands for the sick and the needy who came to these small gatherings for healing. One by one they sat in his big chair and we gathered around them, placing our hands on their heads, backs, arms and legs and allowing the life force to flow through us.

I was amazed to feel my hands warming as we worked.

If, after the healing sessions ended, our energy felt depleted, Sally who had studied *Shiatsu* (Japanese for finger pressure) would lay us down on the carpet and give us brief treatments. I felt far too embarrassed to tell anyone I did healing work, so I followed her lead and took classes so that I could call myself a *Shiatsu* Practitioner and still work with the energy I felt moving through me.

When I heard that a Japanese *Shiatsu* Master was teaching workshops in New York City I resolved to attend.

By that time in my life I had explored many of the world's great cities by day and by night. I had experienced the romance of Paris, the timelessness of Venice, the raw power of Berlin, the tumult of Cairo, the majesty of pre-war Baghdad, and the vastness of Mexico City but I had never been to New York. I loved the creative and vibrant energy of Manhattan and Greenwich Village and the fact that (almost) everyone spoke English!

I took the weekend workshop with *Wataru Ohashi* and when he gave me his *Shiatsu* treatment it felt like an initiation. I knew, from that time on, that I did indeed have a gift and that it would, if necessary, sustain me.

I visited a dear school friend in Venice, California and, on his advice, drove up Highway 1, "to see the redwoods." On the way I visited San Simeon, Big Sur and Monterey Bay and began to feel my heart expanded by the awesome natural beauty I was witnessing.

In October 1980, I found myself in Sausalito, where my hero, Alan Watts, had lived and taught. I imagined a giant circle closing in my life and another one opening as I gazed out into the mist that lay over the San Francisco Bay and listened to the fog horns of the Japanese fishing boats mingling with the barking of the seals as they joined in the herring hunt. I could not bear the thought of leaving that enchanting place, so I rented a room close to the water and printed business cards announcing that I was a *Shiatsu* Practitioner.

Surprise, surprise, the wife in the family of my upstairs neighbors attended a meditation circle. It was held by some graduates of the Berkeley Psychic Institute from whom I learned a valuable technique for staying present and attentive during my practice:

Practice: Grounding with Earth Energy

· *Sit with your hands resting on your thighs palms up.*

· *Become aware of your feet on the floor and imagine the energy of the earth flowing into them, filling them up. You can visualize it as black or brown.*

· *Earth energy flows up from the feet into the ankles, up the legs, through the knees, along the thighs and into the base of the spine.*

· *Now picture a strong, golden cord, with a large crystal attached to the end, extending your spine down through the chair, into the floor, through the foundations of the building and into the earth. It reaches below all the natural root systems and human construction, into the rocky crust of the earth and continues its journey down through the water, gas and molten metal of the mantle of the earth and into the solid, magnetic iron core of the planet where it connects itself into a particular place reserved solely for you. You can even see your name inscribed there.*

· *You belong on this planet. You are safe here.*

· *The earth energy now runs in through your feet, up your legs and thighs and down the golden cord, into the center of the globe.*

· *See it circulating.*

Use this practice whenever your feel spaced-out, disconnected and, particularly (as I attempt to remember) after you have lost your temper.

"What one does not trouble to find within

will not be discovered

by transporting the body

hither and yon."

Chapter Five

Searching for Self-Realization

When my tourist visa ran out I went to see a lawyer who told me to do nothing. Nothing is something I have learned, over the years, to do quite well. I had no official papers so I walked a lot and took my *Shiatsu* mat on the bus.

In 1982 I moved to Mill Valley and there, one day, on the street, I was introduced to Marc Allen, author, publisher and New Age musician (who went on to publish Deepak Chopra and Eckhart Tolle). He hired me to run his fledgeling record company and I ultimately became involved in the early development of the New Age Music business and served on the committee which selected the candidates for the New Age Grammy. I was heavily invested in a music distribution project, working with the major record and book chains, when things went suddenly, horribly wrong and I lost my fortune, my relationship (and my ride) almost overnight.

I fled back down to Los Angeles, staying with my old school friend and his growing family, serving, for a year, as nanny to his 2-year-old, gradually recovering from my trauma and re-emerging as a *Shiatsu* Practitioner. I was out promoting myself through the gyms, spas and beauty salons of Marina-del-Rey when I encountered Carol, a smart, funny, angular, Marlboro Light-smoking yoga instructor. We developed a friendship which bordered on, but never quite achieved, true intimacy. Then, one day, quite out of the blue, she offered to marry me for one year so I could get my Green Card. I was, and still am, so grateful for her generosity of spirit, and to the ease with which the process worked for me, at a time before the immigration laws were changed, in the early 90s.

She also gave me a copy of "The Autobiography of a Yogi" by Paramahansa Yogananda, a great master from India who lived and taught in the West from the 1920s through the 1950s and founded the Self-Realization Fellowship. It is a profound and magical book which inspired me to become a regular visitor to the Lake Shrine Temple, tucked quietly away where busy, winding Sunset Boulevard meets the Pacific Ocean. The garden is a sanctuary of serene beauty where swans and koi swim in a large lake and one can walk the surrounding pathway and be in contemplation or quiet conversation.

I came to understand the importance of creating a physical space in my home which I returned to again and again for regular practice, particularly while having to contend with life in the bustling city.

Practice: Meditation for Self-Realization

· *Sit comfortably in a straight chair with feet firmly planted, thighs and chin parallel to the floor and an erect spine.*

· *Rest your hands on your thighs, close to the body with palms up.*

· *Breathe in and hold your breath, tighten your whole body, tense your thighs, legs and feet, make fists, hunch your shoulders, clench your jaw and squeeze your eyes shut.*

· *Release and breath out making the sound "Huh-huh," the first syllable short and the second long.*

· *Repeat this process 5 times.*

- *When you have completed 5 repetitions, begin to breathe naturally. Just let the breath flow.*

- *Close the eyes and concentrate on a point just above the junction of the eyebrows. It may just be dark or you may see light there. If you do see any light, concentrate on its center.*

- *You may even see the Spiritual Eye, also known as the Cave of Stillness. It has 3 parts, just like the human eye. On the outside is a golden ring, inside the ring, the "iris" color is indigo and the "pupil" inside that, is a white 5- pointed star with the mid-point up.*

- *Now breathe normally in a relaxed way and just be still and focused on the 3rd eye for a 20 minute meditation.*

GIFTS OF MEDITATION

"To eat is to survive to be hungry."

Chapter Six

Vision Quest

By the early 90s I appeared to be doing quite well in life. I had become an American citizen and developed a thriving *Shiatsu* practice. I maintained an office inside my local metaphysical bookstore, called *Vision Quest*, and was working in a nearby chiropractor's office several days a week, mostly on whiplash, caused by low speed car crashes on the crowded California freeways. I was, however, feeling vaguely unhappy and stuck, when an insightful friend took me to meet Samantha at her home in an upscale trailer park overlooking the Pacific Ocean. Now in her 80s, she is a tall, radiant, raven-haired, inspirational and highly intuitive woman. She began her ministry in 1984, when she founded the Spiritual Science Center of Malibu.

Samantha sat me down and conducted a Native American healing ritual, enveloping me in clouds of sage smoke and chanting blessings over me. One of the first exercises she had me do was to sit at my desk for 3 days in a row and write for 6 hours each day. As I wrote it began to feel as though I was emptying the entire contents of my mind onto paper, and when I was done I burned the whole stack. That helped relieve my funk.

We met regularly for brunch at a restaurant that sits on the beach and watched the tourists on the sand, the surf, the seagulls wheeling over the old pier, and we began a friendship which has lasted 25 years. I supported her while she mourned the passing of her husband, her big old red setter, her sister and a male companion, all within a couple of years.

Samantha has a wonderful gift for conducting guided meditations, so when I began to teach my first meditation classes at *Vision Quest*, I invited her to join me. I would lead the group into a relaxed and receptive state through light yoga, some deep breathing, grounding exercises and the *chakra* meditation practice I describe below, and then she would take us on an uplifting journey into higher realms. I was learning about partnership and was about to receive my greatest lessons in its benefits and pitfalls.

Practice: Chakra Meditation

The ancient texts of the East describe 7 energy vortices along the length of the spinal column called "chakras" or spinning wheels of light. Each chakra is associated with an aspect of human consciousness, a corresponding symbol and a color of the light spectrum.

This is an exercise to clear and balance each one in turn:

· *The 1st (root) chakra is located at the base of the spine. Here lies the seat of our basic animal drives for food, shelter and warmth, represented by the square or cube. Breathe into this energy center and picture a beautiful red rosebud opening into full, lustrous bloom there.*

· *The 2nd chakra is 3 finger-widths below the*

*navel. It is our sexual and emotional center,
represented by the triangle or pyramid.
Breathe into this energy center and picture a
beautiful orange rosebud opening into full,
lustrous bloom there.*

· *The 3rd chakra is at the solar plexus, just
below the ribcage. This is the center of our
intuition and personal power in the world,
represented by the circle or sphere. Breathe
into this energy center and picture a beautiful
yellow rosebud opening into full, lustrous
bloom there.*

· *The 4th chakra is the heart center. This is the
seat of unconditional love, represented by the
equilateral cross. Breathe into this energy
center and picture a beautiful green rosebud
opening into full, lustrous bloom there.*

· *The 5th chakra is in the throat. It is the
communication center, represented by the*

crescent. Breathe into this energy center and picture a beautiful light blue rosebud opening into full, lustrous bloom there.

• The 6th chakra is the 3rd eye, just above the junction of the eyebrows. It is the center of inner vision, represented by the 5-pointed star with the mid-point up. Breathe into this energy center and picture a beautiful indigo rosebud opening into full lustrous bloom there.

• The 7th (crown) chakra is above the top of the head. It is the seat of our connectedness to the Source of All That Is, represented by the lotus flower with a thousand petals. Breathe into this energy center and picture a beautiful violet lotus flower opening into full lustrous bloom there.

• You can open and close the roses or the lotus flower. If you are picking up unwanted *energies, close the lotus flower in your crown chakra.*

· *If any of the chakras feel too wide open, close them back into a bud.*

· *Restoring the picture of a colored bloom will keep the chakra clean.*

· *Sit quietly and breathe gently for one minute more, and then end your meditation.*

"When all the ideas of self-power based on moral values and disciplinary measures are purged, there is nothing left in you that will declare itself to be the hearer, and just because of this, you do not miss anything you hear."

Chapter Seven

Affirming the Affirmative

One of the most powerful lessons I learned from Samantha was that the writing and verbal repetition of life-affirming statements can re-program the mind with the truth of who we truly are and improve our health, financial well-being, sense of purpose and general morale.

I have devoted this chapter to affirmations, not because they are a meditation in themselves, but because they helped me to improve the quality of my life and, if you repeat them quietly to yourself while in a meditative state, they may enter more deeply into your consciousness and be an effective tool for transforming your world.

It has become increasingly clear to me, as the years have unfolded, that our thoughts, whether conscious or unconscious, create our reality.

Most of the time we are not in control of, or even aware of the ideas that are coursing through our minds and running our lives. Often we indulge ourselves in negative self-talk. We tell ourselves we are not enough, that we are unloveable or unintelligent, that we will always be unhealthy or unable to sustain ourselves. We give our power away to others who may be acting out of their own self-interest. We believe the words of those who do not know anything about us and certainly have no earthly reason to care about our fate.

I repeated the affirmations Samantha gave me with religious fervor. I switched off the rock n' roll on my car radio and chanted as I drove.   I mumbled them as I hiked in the hills, said them to myself as I stared into the bathroom mirror and as I lay in bed, morning and evening. My self-image began to improve, my confidence grew and I was gradually able to imagine myself creating a better and more fulfilling life.

Within a few weeks one of my clients told her friend and employer about me and my work, and my life was changed forever. It felt as though my affirmations had created Judy, just as her prayers for a new love in her life created me.

Judy, an experienced retailer, had recently opened her 3rd store, *The Imagine Center*, a metaphysical book, gift and healing center, and "urban oasis" selling "sacred treasures" on busy Ventura Boulevard in the middle of the San Fernando Valley. We met and felt an immediate and strong bond. We discovered that our fathers were born just weeks apart, were both WWII veterans and leaders in their respective Jewish communities. We made each other laugh out loud, happened to be reading the same inspiring, metaphysical books at the same time and we started to spend almost all our free time together.

The owners of *Vision Quest* were in the process of moving out of town and we saw this as a perfect opportunity to begin to work together. I moved my practice to *The Imagine Center* and taught meditation classes there. Ultimately I became Judy's husband, junior partner and C.E.O. of her retail empire.

We spent the next 17 years together, a rich but not an easy time. In spite of our similarities we are very different characters and we went through some challenging times. Long hours in the therapist's office, working on issues within ourselves and with each other, inevitably ended in forgiveness and a reminder of the love that had brought us and kept us together.

I was able to continue on my spiritual journey, read, learn, grow and become a *Reiki* Master and Minister. We became part of a joyful community in Los Angeles and traveled happily together throughout North America, Europe (primarily Italy, where we had both lived) Asia and, of course, the Hawaiian Islands.

In 2009 we migrated to Maui together but soon went our separate ways. She owns metaphysical stores in Haiku, upcountry, and in Kihei, along the ocean front, and we continue our fond and faithful friendship.

I was learning that there is a time to persevere and a time to let go and that our emotions are signposts along the way. By tuning in to, and surrendering to my true heart's desire, I am now fully confident that I will always be led towards my highest good.

Practice: Affirmations

Here are a few of my favorite affirmations to work with. Use them or write your own using this format. Write each one that you choose 100 times.

Make them specific to an issue you are working on, personally applicable to you by inserting your name whenever possible and keep them in the present tense by using the word "now." Remember that the past has gone and the future is yet to be. All that really exists is "an infinity of nowness." The present, The Holy Moment, is your only point of true power.

Repeat each affirmation out loud throughout the day, whenever you look into a mirror and silently to yourself when you are in an expanded state at the end of your meditation practice:

"I, (insert your name) am now creating perfect health in a fit and energized body."

"All my needs are abundantly met, more than I can ever imagine."

"In and easy and relaxed manner, in a healthy and positive way, all the money I want and need is coming to me, in its own perfect time, for the highest good of all."

"I am happy, I am healthy, I am prospering, I am safe."

"Every day, in every way, I am getting better and better."

"I love and approve of myself."

"I trust my inner light and intuition to guide me."

"I choose to see my family as a gift."

......and, when (apparent) misfortune or disaster strikes...........

"Only good can come from this."

I began this short book with a breathing exercise and I will conclude with one. Judy and I learned this breath while studying Techniques of Tantra in a rustic resort on the coast of Mexico, where the beds were suspended from the ceiling and swung gently as we slept. The practices that we learned turned out to be as much about controlling the breath and attaining higher states of consciousness as about increasing ones level of physical intimacy. I recommend this breath for centering and focusing the attention before meditation:

Practice: The Seven-Fold Breath

- *Breathe in through the nose to the count of 7.*

- *Hold the full breath in, with full lungs, to the count of 7.*

- *Exhale fully through the mouth, to the count of 7.*

- *Hold the breath out, with empty lungs, to the count of 7.*

- *Repeat this entire process 7 times.*

GIFTS OF MEDITATION

MICHAEL J. DAWSON

"The breath is the bridge

Between the soul and the self."

Epilogue

There is no mystery to meditation, no great secret. Do not fall into the trap of imagining that simply because you cannot stop your mind from thinking, or your body from itching and twitching, you cannot be successful at sitting quietly in contemplation.

Even the most experienced meditators have busy thoughts, but they have learned, little by little, to let them be. They cease to identify with them and, instead, gradually withdraw from them in order to move towards a state of *witness consciousness*.

The ever-chattering *monkey mind* is quite expert at doing its job. It generates a constant procession of thoughts and then examines them from this angle and that angle, turns them upside down and inside out. It continually analyses, compares and judges. It regrets the past and worries about the future.

Our minds may be useful tools for navigating the way through a world of 3 dimensions but they do not define who we are are. We are not our personalities, the work we do or the names that our parents and societies gave to us. We are infinite awareness beyond form. We are universal consciousness having an experience of being human, a point of attention within infinite possibility.

We are taught to value the intellect, but my own consistently wretched experiences in the classrooms of my youth taught me to be suspicious of it. Knowledge is not wisdom. A quick glance around the planet should be enough to prove that point!

When we come to the end of our journey, and the issues that so concerned us recede from us like the day before the coming night, it will be the love we have offered that will become our legacy to the universe.

I have poured the history of my heart into this telling of my tale. My prayer is that it gives impetus to a desire within your heart to take a few moments of out of each day, temper the drive to do, to accomplish, and briefly surrender to the awareness that something higher and greater actually does exist and that it is within every soul's capacity to connect with it.

Bibliography

"The Way of Zen" by Alan Watts

"Memories, Dreams Reflections ," by Carl Jung

"The Secret of the Golden Flower," translated by Richard Wilhelm

"Zen Shiatsu" by Shizuto Masunaga and Wataru Ohashi

"Autobiography of a Yogi" by Paramahansa Yogananda

"Bringers of the Dawn" and *"Earth"* by Barbara Marciniak

GIFTS OF MEDITATION

MICHAEL J. DAWSON

Made in the USA
San Bernardino, CA
16 November 2013